AGUSTÍN BARRIOS MANGORÉ

UN SUEÑO en la FLORESTA

For Solo Guitar

Edited by Richard D. Stover

Biography Of Agustín Barrios Mangoré

Agustín Pío Barrios (b. May 5, 1885, d. August 7, 1944) was the greatest virtuoso guitarist/composer of the first half of the present century. Born in the small town of San Juan Bautista de las Misiones in Paraguay into a large family which esteemed both music and literature, he began to play the guitar at a very early age. He received his primary education in a Jesuit school where he utilized his guitar in the study of harmony. His first formal instructor, Gustavo Sosa Escalda, introduced young Agustín to the Sor and Aguado methods, as well as pieces by Tárrega, Viñas, Arcas, and Parga. By the age of 13 he was recognized as a prodigy and given a scholarship to the Colegio Nacional in Asunción where, in addition to music, he distinguished himself in mathematics, journalism and literature. He also studied calligraphy and was a talented graphic artist.

Barrios, a great lover of culture, was quoted as having said, "One cannot become a guitarist if he has not bathed in the fountain of culture." In addition to Spanish he also spoke *Guaraní*, the native tongue of Paraguay. He read French, English and German and was keenly interested in philosophy, poetry and theosophy. He exercised daily and enjoyed working out on the high bar. He was warm, kind-hearted and spontaneous. Musically he was a tremendous improviser, and many stories are told of his completely spontaneous improvisations (many times in concert). His astounding creative facility enabled him to compose over 300 works for the guitar!

In his music we find truly inspired creativity combined with a total technical dominion of the guitar's harmonic capabilities. His knowledge of harmonic science enabled him to compose in several styles: baroque, classic, romantic and descriptive. He composed preludes, studies, suites, waltzes, mazurkas, tarantellas and romanzas, as well as many onomatopoetic works describing physical objects or historical/cultural themes. His most famous piece, *Diana Guaraní,* reenacted the War of the Triple Alliance which took place in Paraguay in 1864, complete with cannons, horses, drums, marching, and explosions! He also played a good deal of popular music, many of his finest compositions based on the song and dance forms found throughout Iberoamerica (cueca, choro, estilo, maxixe, milonga, pericón, tango, zamba and zapateado).

In 1932 he began to bill himself as "Nitsuga Mangoré — the Pagannini of the Guitar from the Jungles of Paraguay." Nitsuga (Agustín spelled backwards) and Mangoré (a legendary Guaraní chieftain who resisted the Spanish conquest) were used by Barrios for several years, after which he dropped this pseudonym to become simply Agustín Barrios Mangoré.

In addition to Paraguay, Barrios lived in Argentina, Uruguay, Brazil, Venezuela, Costa Rica and El Salvador. In these countries, as well as Chile, Mexico, Guatemala, Honduras, Panamá, Colombia, Cuba, Haití, Dominican Republic and Trinidad, he concertized continually from 1910 till his death. From 1934-'36 he was in Europe, playing in Belgium, Germany, Spain and England.

Perhaps over a hundred of his works still survive, either in manuscript or on the many 78 rpm records he made (over 30 records on 4 different labels). In addition to his own works, he played hundreds of other pieces, including all the standard works in the guitar repertoire up to that time (transcriptions of Bach, Haydn, Mozart, Beethoven, Chopin, Albéniz, Granados, as well as works of Sor, Aguado, Giuliani, Costé, Tárrega, Tórroba and Turina).

One can appreciate in Barrios Mangoré a logical expansion of techniques defined by masters such as Sor and Tárrega, carried to an even higher level of expressiveness and technical expertise. The legacy of his genius is a priceless one for all lovers of the guitar.

Richard Stover

Un Sueño en la Floresta

AGUSTÍN BARRIOS MANGORÉ
Edited by RICHARD D. STOVER

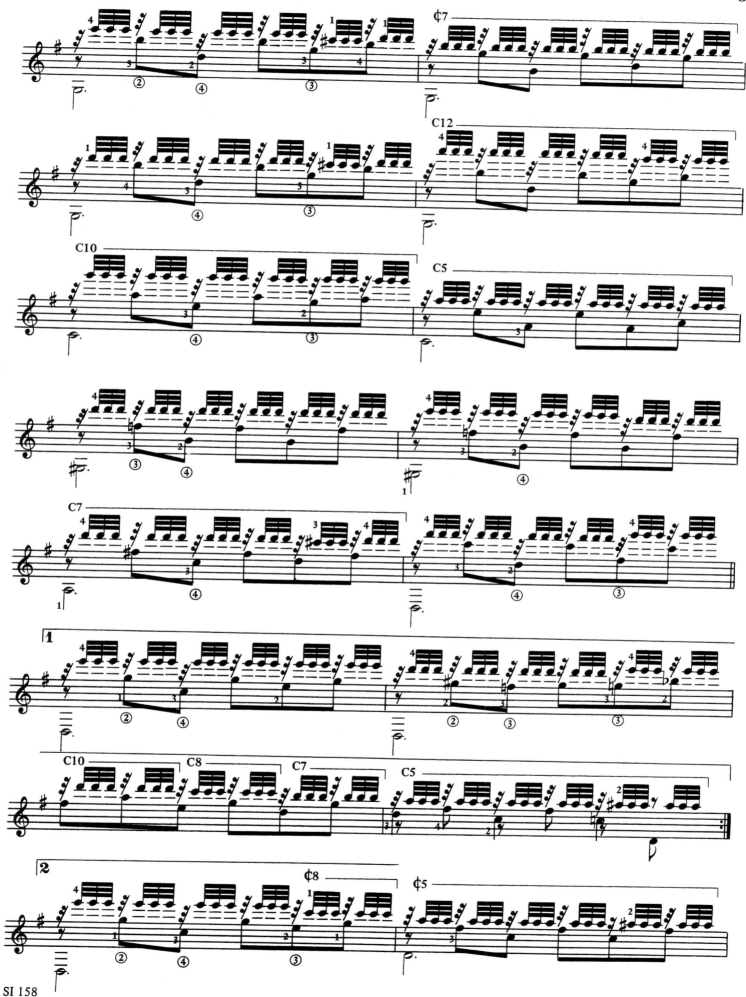

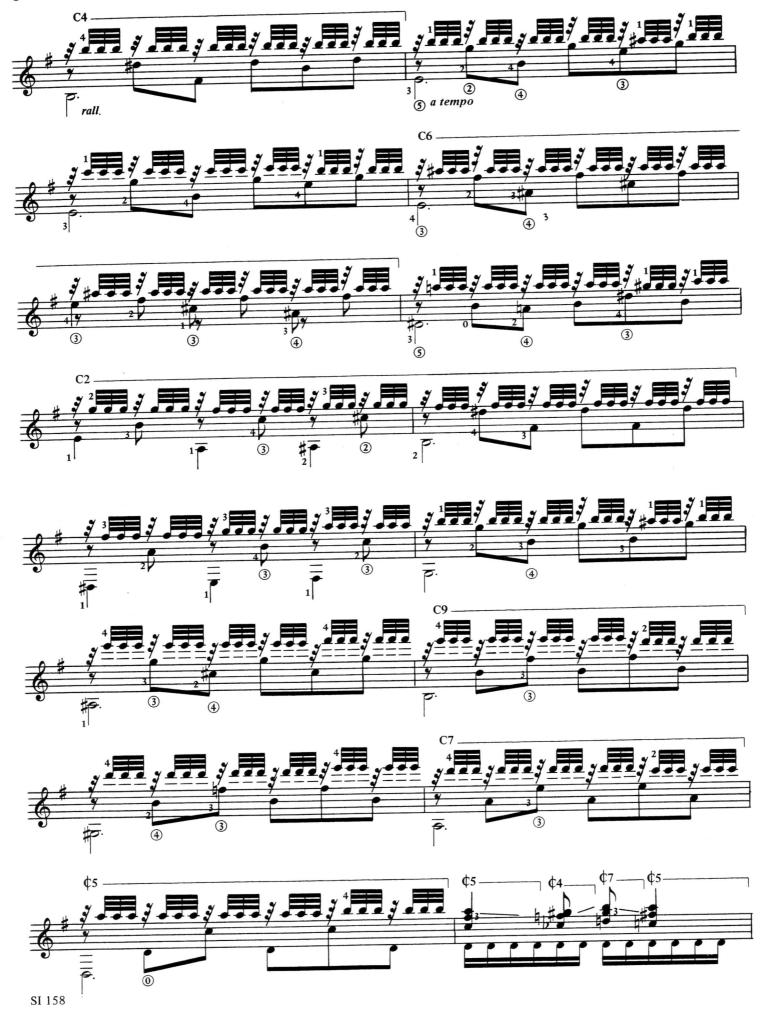

(Optional variation)

8

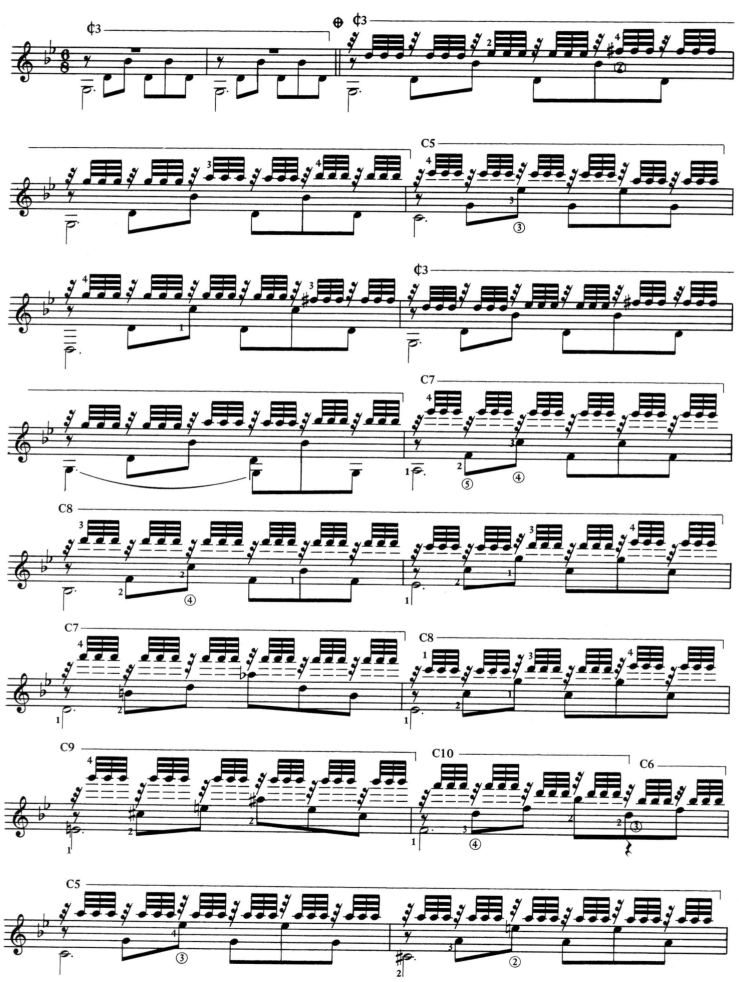

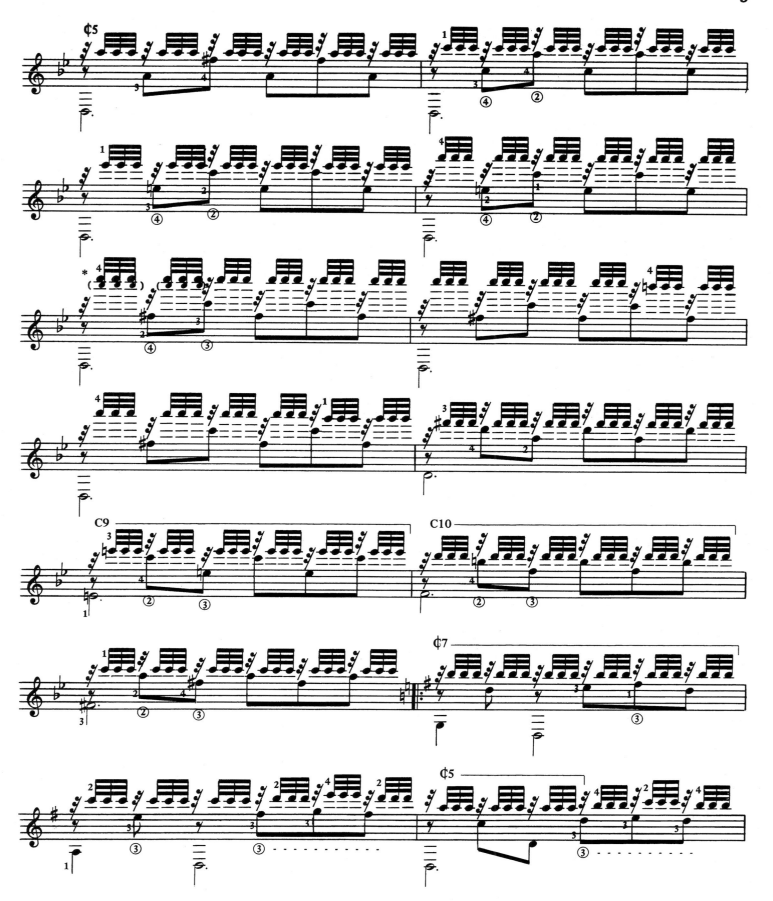

*To play this high C a 20th frett is required (the DiGiorgio guitar on which Barrios created this piece had such an additional frett). In lieu of such, an A can be substituted as suggested in parenthesis.

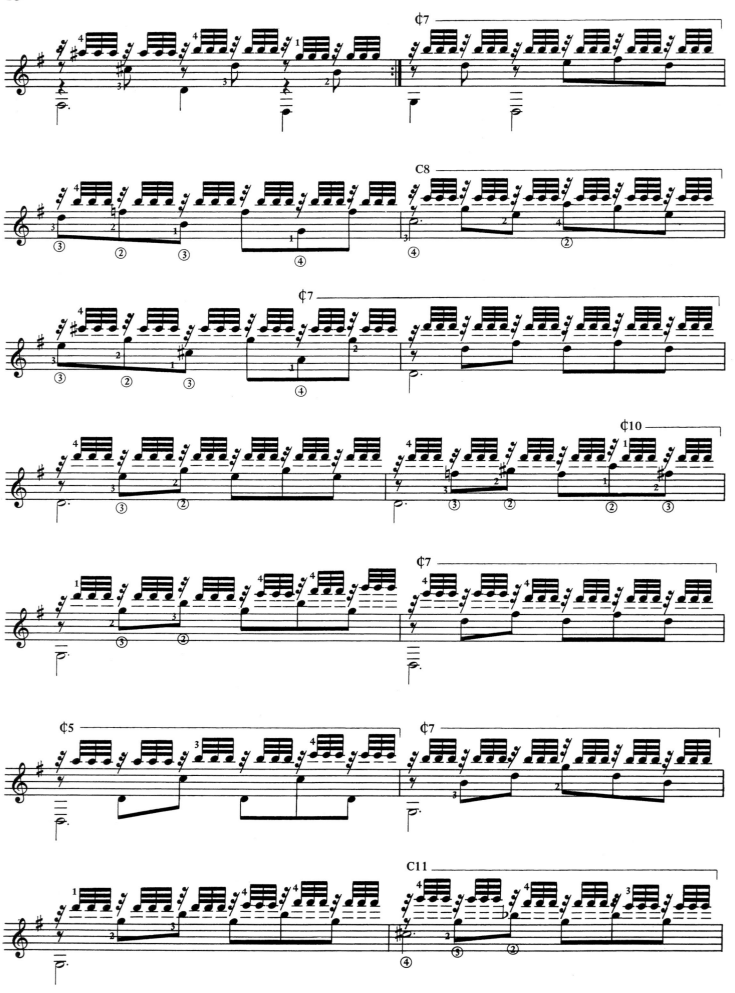

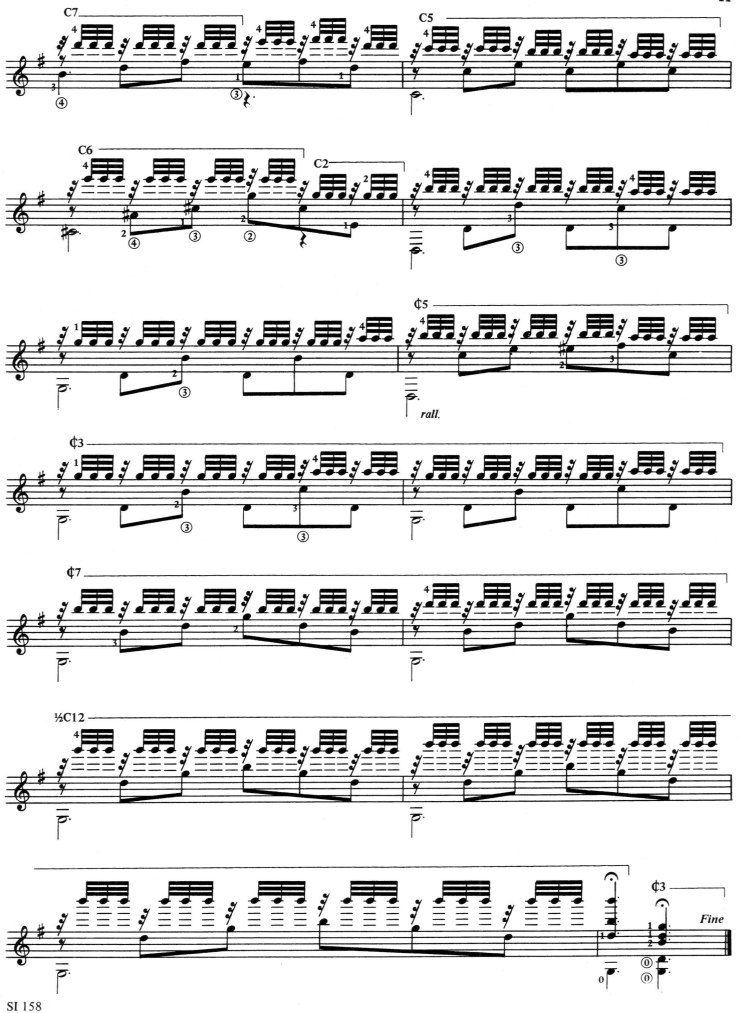